# The CIVILITY Workout

## Your Personal Guide to Unleashing Civility in the Workplace

# DIANA DAMRON

© Diana Damron 2017 / WarLee House Publishing

PO Box 2675
Kalispell, MT 59903
(406) 890-8453

Diana@DianaDamron.com
www.dianadamron.com

C's the Day® is a registered trademark of WarLee House Publishing.

Graphic design by Brenda Hawkes

Edited by Phyllis Jask

Author photos by B. Victoria Wojciechowski

Printed in the United States of America

ISBN-13: 978-0998934204

# PRAISE FOR *CIVILITY UNLEASHED*

*Every day, customers define your company by the civility of its employees! Ask yourself, what do customers see in your employees? Do customers line up to do business or run for the exits? Diana Damron's solutions represent a fresh way of thinking. Follow her custom, self-guiding path to a more profitable, efficient, and effective civil work environment!*

> **—Stephen P. Behringer, Procter & Gamble Senior Sales Technology Manager, Kmart Senior Vice President**

*Caught up in a toxic work environment? It can affect your life and attitude both on and off the job. Diana Damron has penned the book to help you diagnose your situation, evaluate your position, and assess your next steps. She sets forth a helpful approach to analyzing the causes of workplace incivility, and provides intuitive and introspective analysis of possible causes and steps to be taken to correct the condition, and perhaps most importantly, to protect yourself.*

> **—David A. Ogden, Attorney at Law, and inspiration for the book *The Lincoln Lawyer***

# CONTENTS

# INTRODUCTION

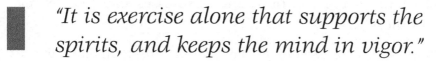

*"It is exercise alone that supports the
spirits, and keeps the mind in vigor."*

—Marcus Tullium Cicero

The need for civility has never been more urgent, so the fact that you
want to develop and exercise your civil self is exciting news.

Day after day, we are dealing with a crisis in trust. We don't trust the
government, the media, or business. And from a quick scan of social
media, we're not particularly trusting of some of our friends, family, or
colleagues either.

So why bring up trust when our focus is on civility? Because the two
are interdependent. If you don't have civility, you don't have trust.
If you don't have trust you don't have the vital ingredient to every
relationship—whether it's your relationship with your leadership, your
direct reports, or your colleagues. No matter whether the relationship is
with your client, your friend, or your partner, if it's not built on trust—
ongoing trust—it's not healthy.

When you don't have trust—there's a reason: **you don't have civility!**

We, as a society, have twisted ourselves into a knot trying to figure out
how to cooperate, live together harmoniously, and produce magnificent
goods and services. While we've made a commitment to these lofty
goals, we haven't made the same commitment to civility! Yet, each of
these goals requires that you and I exercise civility consistently.

## THE 3 C'S CONNECTION

As I explained in *Civility Unleashed: Using Civility to Survive and Thrive in the Workplace,* I run my consulting company on the principle that *You* **Communicate** *your* **Character** *by how you exercise your* **Civility. Let me translate: You and I tell the world** *who* **we are and** *what* **we stand for and what our organizations and businesses stand for by** *how* **we treat others.**

There's nothing in my 10-word tagline or in its translation that indicates you exercise your civility *only* when it's easy, convenient, or when you like and agree with the other person. No! The demand for exercising civility is ongoing. Day in and day out, week in and week out, year in and year out. You must be civil to the other person—no matter whether they agree with you, sound like you, or behave like you. As well, you must also be civil to yourself.

Like any athlete who wants to score more goals, win more games, and walk away in victory, it takes practice. Top athletes practice their skills over and over again until it becomes natural—until it becomes a habit. Civility is no different. We must exercise civility over and over again— even in stressful crunch times, even with our competition, and even when it seems impossible—to create the habit.

If *how* we exercise civility reveals to the world who we truly are at our core, it's vital that we exercise civility repeatedly to create a habitual reaction. Our goal is to exercise civility regardless of our relationship to another person, regardless of whether it's convenient, and regardless of whether it's easy. In other words, we must be intentional and rigorous about exercising our civility muscles.

### Civility Unmasked

Civility—for far too many people—is a word that is misunderstood, undervalued, and even tossed aside. Yes, the term finds itself in the headlines and into conversations and accusations, but unfortunately, it doesn't find itself in use. So let's begin by clarifying just what civility is.

Civility is the *consistent* communication of respect, as demonstrated through politeness and courtesy, whether or not you like the other person, and whether or not you agree with the other person.

If you notice, the definition is a bit different than how I defined it in *Civility Unleashed*. Please allow me to explain.

My original definition fell short, I feel, in two areas. Number one: I needed to answer the question, "So, how **do** I communicate respect for the other person when I know that his/her behavior is such that I can't respect it?" First, you show politeness and courtesy to that individual because they're a *human being*. Second, you're respectful and polite because of the role they play: he or she is your boss, a family member, or holds a *position* of respect. (After all, you want to keep your job so you can pay the mortgage and buy groceries, you want to keep peace in your family, or the position itself is one of great responsibility and value to others—even if you don't agree with the person who currently holds it.)

Number two, we are increasingly becoming a society that destroys those with whom we disagree—whether on social media, in conversation, or in life. As Mahatma Gandhi said, "The weak can never forgive. Forgiveness is the attribute of the strong. An eye for an eye ends up making the whole world blind."[1] Whether or not we agree or even like each other, we must learn to treat one another with courtesy.

## STRENGTH, HEART, AND RESILIENCE THROUGH CIVILITY

I consider one of the most critical reasons for being relentless about demanding civility in one's self is the power it instills within and inspires outward. Anyone, yours truly included, stuck in a toxic environment knows the feeling of having no control. Someone else not only seems to seize control of your day, but of you personally—your emotions, your thinking, and your well-being. It's time to take back control—to seize the day.

The Latin phrase, carpe diem, means "Seize the Day!" I want you to have that feeling, that sense that **you** are in control of your day and that you are going to squeeze everything good, great, and wonderful out of the day. And what better way than by treating yourself and others with respect!

Throughout the book, you'll see my own personal take on that expression: **C's the Day**®. As your coach, I'll ask you to pause and take part in **C's the Day**® Exercises. They're to elucidate, enlighten, and embolden you. I want you to **C's your Day**!

### Commitment to Civility

If you've ever committed to a workout regimen, you probably had a specific goal in mind, like losing 10 pounds to lower your cholersterol. You not only want to be around for your kids and grandkids, but you want to be able to scurry after them; you want to feel better throughout the day and sleep through the night without tossing and turning; or you just want to look smashing at your high school reunion. (And I'm not just talking to you ladies!) With your goal in mind, you made a pledge to get stronger, healthier, and more flexible.

With this book in hand, you're making a commitment to develop your civil self. That means an entirely new exercise program—one that's different from anything you've found yourself participating in before. You're going to be exercising *civility*—learning how to strengthen your civility muscles. As you discovered in chapter 11 of *Civility Unleashed*, that means a change in focus.

You're going to focus on civility—your own civility toward others and your civility toward yourself. While that may sound a bit confusing right now, it will become clearer as you work through the exercises in this workbook.

## *I'm Here for You*

This book is your indispensable companion to *Civility Unleashed: Using Civility to Survive and Thrive in the Workplace.* Your ally is this pair of books—whether you're caught in a toxic environment, you're a leader trying to figure out how to create and maintain a culture of trust, or you just want to unleash more civility in your own life.

I'll push you when you're ready to throw in the towel, I'll hold you accountable when you want to take the easy and *uncivil* way out, and I'll applaud you as you build the civil musculature that will be the envy— and the role model—for your culture and community.

*The Civility Workout* is small so that you can squeeze it into your computer bag, your purse, or your backpack. You can slide it into the top drawer of your desk or keep it front and center. The idea is to keep *The Civility Workout* close by. It's your buddy for moral support, double-checking your sanity (yes, I mean exactly that), and quickly reviewing an important lesson.

## *How to use* The Civility Workout

*The Civility Workout i*s for you to put into practice the lessons you learned in *Civility Unleashed.* You'll create goals and then hold yourself accountable. You'll track what works and what doesn't work for you. You'll turn to *The Civility Workout* to journal your triggers and those of others and how to best deal with them. Maybe you'll pull out the Workout for a quick refresher. As you watch your scores rise in the Civility Quotient Assessments, you'll begin to see that you're creating habits that generate and unleash civility. And that means—you're building **trust!**

Use this workbook in a way that works best for you! If you want to keep it to yourself, you're welcome to privacy. If you want to partner with someone on this excursion, find a workout partner that you trust, and carry on.

*Civility Unleashed* prompts ideas, gives case studies, and provides tools. *The Civility Workout* is for you to put into practice what you are learning.

With that in mind, let's begin to **C's the Day**, and dive into *The Civility Workout*.

## NOTES INTRODUCTION

[1]    Henrick Edberg, "Gandhi's 10 Rules for Changing the World," Daily Good, available at http://www.dailygood.org/story/466/gandhi-s-10-rules-for-changing-the-world-henrik-edberg/.

# PART I: STRENGTH

# WE'RE OPEN FOR BUSINESS

> *"I know it's sappy, but I bet there's a market for civility and niceness out there that, while probably not as titillating as a junkyard scrap between shirtless adversaries, it'd sure be healthier."*
>
> —Steven Weber

Welcome to the **civility gym!** Don't worry, there's no expensive gym equipment to purchase, trendy workout clothes to buy, or even monthly dues to pay. There's just you and me, and your companion book *Civility Unleashed: Using Civility to Survive and Thrive in the Workplace.*

I've broken the workout into four components: **Strength, Cardio, Flexibility,** and **Diet**. These are the same four elements of any workout; however, this approach will be different from lifting barbells, running on a treadmill, or holding a yoga pose. *The Civility Workout's* strength, cardio, flexibility, and diet pieces will be just as demanding—if not more. As with a traditional physical workout, you build endurance, strength, and a better version of you! In the civility gym, you develop a stronger, more heart-based, more flexible, and more nourished civil self.

### Your Goal

Before we go any further, I'd like you to take a moment to pause and consider one thing: Why are you here? What is your goal? When you have a clear-cut goal in front of you, it's easier to hit your target. You're more willing to do the work and ditch the excuses. So pause and think about why you're ready to dive into this workout.

Perhaps you have more than one goal. For example, professionally, you may want to be a better leader—one who connects more effectively with your team. You may also have a personal goal to be more gracious, affectionate, and appreciative of members of your own family. Go ahead and write multiple goals. However, if you do, what is the one that is going to be the goal that you have front and center right now? What is the goal that is the most important for you to reach immediately? Ready? Write!

**GOALS:** (Feel free to label them as personal or professional.)

_____

_____

_____

_____

_____

_____

_____

_____

Good job! You've written down your goals. Once you've identified the one you want to work on right now, don't hesitate to plaster that goal everywhere—on your bathroom mirror, inside your top drawer at work, below your computer screen, on your dashboard, inside a kitchen cabinet door, on your treadmill. Email or text that goal to yourself. Schedule it to pop up on your daily calendar. Put your goal someplace where you see it daily. Seeing it regularly should help you move through the obstacles that will pop up, enticing you to give up and take the easy way out. Stay strong and endure!

Now, on to your core work!

## ZEROING IN ON YOUR CORE

 *"A core value is one you're willing to get punished for."*

—Patrick Lencioni

Increasingly, fitness trainers tell us to focus on our core—abdominals, lower back, hips, and pelvis. Think sit-ups and planks. Why? As we strengthen our core, we begin to improve our balance and stability. A strong core makes other athletic endeavors and exercises easier.

It's much the same in *The Civility Workout*. As you work to strengthen your core, you begin to improve your mental and emotional balance and stability. You'll find yourself stronger in the midst of change or drama. You'll remain well-balanced, weighing the arguments rather than reacting emotionally to triggers. You'll be more resilient and less timid.

In terms of your core and its role in the civil self, think about your core values. Those are the beliefs that help you decide right from wrong. Your core values drive your personal behaviors. In terms of your professional life, they're the values that drive the behaviors in your corporate culture. Or they should.

When your personal life syncs with your professional values—you are manifesting your best civil self.

## DETERMINE YOUR CORE VALUES

Core values are critical to how you see yourself, how you see others, and how you either seize the day or let the day wrestle you to the ground before you walk out your front door.

Your core values serve as your guides and inspirations. They provide your measure for success. They create your vision.

Below is a list of values that may describe your own core values:

- Family
- Faith
- Loyalty
- Trust
- Truth
- Integrity
- Honesty
- Industriousness
- Cooperation
- Joy
- Service

- Generosity
- Security
- Dependability
- Open-Mindedness
- Creativity
- Success
- Adventure
- Fun
- Inspiration
- Passion

Please look at the list above. See if some of these core values ring true for you. Or add your own. There are three steps in this exercise:

**Step one.** Find or choose 10 words from above that sincerely speak to the way you want to live your life and the way you want to conduct business. Again, you may want to come up with a few of your own.

_____        _____

_____        _____

_____        _____

_____        _____

_____        _____

**Step two.** Whittle your list down to five core values and review them to see how they mesh with both your personal and professional lives.

_____

_____

_____

_____

_____

**Step three.** Now, select three **core values** that reflect your standards and the code of conduct you hold most dear. When your behavior and communication don't align with your core values, it's time to make an adjustment.

_____

_____

_____

### Benchmarking through Core Values

Good work! You've determined your core values. It's these final three values you've selected that you'll use to benchmark your work and progress in developing your civility muscles.

With your core values in mind, let's head into the weight room.

## BUILDING STRENGTH THROUGH YOUR CIVIL CORE

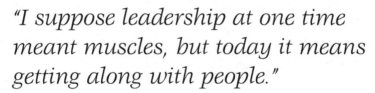

*"I suppose leadership at one time meant muscles, but today it means getting along with people."*

—Mahatma Gandhi

Imagine you've just stepped into a busy weight room. You look around and find yourself surrounded by people lifting barbells and dumbbells. Everyone is here to build muscle. Whether you choose free weights, a resistance band, or a machine that demands pushing or pulling, your objective is to get stronger. The weights are measures of resistance, and as you get stronger, you'll be able to lift or push increased levels of resistance.

It's not much different when it comes to the civility gym. You're dealing with resistance, but your resistance doesn't come in the form of free weights; it usually comes in the form of a person or team that resists change, resists respectful behavior, resists ethical standards, and resists collaboration. Maybe they just resist cooperating with you in a manner that you find acceptable. That person or group of people may be among your peers, your direct reports, your customers, or your leadership. Or as unpleasant as the thought may be, the resistance may even be stemming from you!

Your ability to lift greater weight—to deal with increasing resistance— will grow as you develop a stronger understanding of what civility is and what it demands of you. Once you get stronger and are used to dealing with resistance, you'll feel more comfortable flexing your civility muscles.

We'll begin your workout by determining how strong you are now. Can you lift a 200-pound barbell or a two-pound dumbbell?

## CIVILITY QUOTIENT ASSESSMENT—STRENGTH

As you go through each statement, please circle 1 if you think you need a lot of work or you don't consider this a priority. Circle 5 if you think you excel in this area. Of the 18 questions, there's the potential for a low score of 18 and a high score of 90.

| | | | | | |
|---|---|---|---|---|---|
| I consider civility a high priority. | 1 | 2 | 3 | 4 | 5 |
| I don't take things personally. | 1 | 2 | 3 | 4 | 5 |
| I take a breath before responding—sometimes a really deep breath. | 1 | 2 | 3 | 4 | 5 |
| I am assertive, yet polite. | 1 | 2 | 3 | 4 | 5 |
| I don't walk on eggshells. | 1 | 2 | 3 | 4 | 5 |
| I'm not afraid to tell the truth, even when it's not welcome news. | 1 | 2 | 3 | 4 | 5 |
| I can push back and confront without getting aggressive. | 1 | 2 | 3 | 4 | 5 |
| I can push back and confront without getting personal. | 1 | 2 | 3 | 4 | 5 |
| I push back and confront with poise and control. | 1 | 2 | 3 | 4 | 5 |
| If someone questions my decision, I'm not defensive. | 1 | 2 | 3 | 4 | 5 |
| I'm comfortable asking questions. | 1 | 2 | 3 | 4 | 5 |
| I have no problems asking questions in front of others if I don't understand. | 1 | 2 | 3 | 4 | 5 |
| I can see the humorous side of a situation. | 1 | 2 | 3 | 4 | 5 |
| I make healthy choices to put myself in a better frame of mind. | 1 | 2 | 3 | 4 | 5 |

| | | | | | |
|---|---|---|---|---|---|
| I have the ability to compartmentalize negativity in the workplace. I don't let it drag me into a negative emotional state. | 1 | 2 | 3 | 4 | 5 |
| I turn on some music, dance, or go for a jog to deal with my frustration. | 1 | 2 | 3 | 4 | 5 |
| I don't dwell on the negativity. | 1 | 2 | 3 | 4 | 5 |
| I take full responsibility for my communication and my behavior. | 1 | 2 | 3 | 4 | 5 |

## Scoring

How did you do? I find that most people have two entirely different approaches when taking the Civility Quotient Assessments (CQAs). They're either too hard on themselves and forget that they're human or they're unable to see their behavior for what it is—uncivil.

Take the CQA again. One of the most important skills to cultivate your civil core is to be very clear on your behavior—how you communicate, how you come across, and what triggers both your positive and negative responses.

An extremely helpful strategy is to ask someone whom you trust to review your CQA with you. Do they find you're accurate in your assessment? Clients periodically tell me when they see how a colleague or leader assesses him- or herself, they realize that that individual doesn't have a clue how they're coming across. If this could be you, it's a possible signal to seek one-on-one coaching or mentoring to help strengthen your civil core.

## Take Time for Reflection

With your assessment in hand, you should have an idea of your strength when it comes to your ability to generate trust through exercising civility. Do you have so many 5s on your assessment that your civil musculature would place you in consideration for the cover of *Flex* magazine (a magazine for weight-lifters)?

Or do you have a pile of 1s and 2s? If you're a bit flabby in the areas of polite assertiveness, maintaining self-confidence in the face of push-back, or making healthy choices consistently, commit right now to focusing on those low-score areas.

If you've ever gone long periods without exercise, you know that recommitting to it is neither easy nor painless. After all, "use it or lose it" applies to everything. Sit on the couch eating bonbons and your muscles will ultimately atrophy; movement takes immense effort. It's the same with your civility muscles. If you haven't been using them, you'll lose them. Flexing your civility muscles take work. It takes repetition. And it takes you standing up and refusing to come up with excuses.

Do you have mostly 3s and 4s? It looks like you understand civility. You understand that it leads to trust and is essential in life. You're good—but I'm going to push you to be great. Be the influence that everyone needs to see day in and day out. Show others how to maintain poise in the face of rude behavior, how to stay respectful but assertive in conflict, and how to be healthy and assured even when surrounded by toxicity. You are the power of influence. Keep working at growing and strengthening your civility muscles.

# C's the Day EXERCISE

Please review your lower scores (1s and 2s). Those are the specific areas you need to focus on. Write them here:

_____

_____

_____

_____

_____

Now, zero in on one specific "flabby muscle" of civility at a time. Determine what behaviors, mannerisms, and communication styles you need to target and write them here:

_____

_____

_____

_____

_____

Identify areas you're strong in (4s and 5s). Those strengths enhance your civility and help you generate **trust**.

_____

_____

_____

_____

_____

You're going to need a written plan to successfully strengthen your areas of weakness. Write one or two goals for achieving success in those areas:

_____

_____

_____

_____

_____

**Communicating Character by Exercising Civility**

# C's the Day EXERCISE

What is your biggest obstacle to being strong civility-wise? Be specific. Is it another person? Is it a group of people? Is a policy? Is it your desk? Is it your office? (Are you so frustrated with your desk and physical layout of your office, that it affects your attitude and therefore your communication and the way you behave?) Is it your schedule? Is it the duties you're expected to complete? Is it your company culture? (Picture this person or situation as a barbell laden at each end with heavy weights. If anything, it might add a bit of humor to the situation.)

_____

_____

_____

_____

Why is that barbell (person, thing, or situation) so difficult to manage (e.g., the person's behavior is rude, gruff, overly sweet, loud, tardy, inefficient)? Does that group of people ignore you, gossip, belittle you, etc.? Is your desk a mess, next to someone who is very chatty, or physically uncomfortable? Is your office too dark, too loud, ugly, or crowded? Do you have to get to work too early? Is it hard to schedule your personal obligations with your workplace duties? Is the culture confusing?

_____

_____

_____

_____

_____

You've identified your barbell (source of resistance) and what makes it difficult to manage. What can you do about it to put you in a stronger position (e.g., change or shift your attitude, seek one-on-one coaching or mentoring, make a commitment to embrace your core values, work on your self-confidence, improve your physical demeanor)?

_____

_____

_____

_____

_____

How does that barbell affect you in achieving your goal (e.g., is your schedule so demanding that you're often tired and grumpy? Does your direct report not remember your training? Does your leader micromanage you?)

_____

_____

_____

_____

_____

Are you compromising your core values presently when dealing with this obstacle? Which value and how?

_____

_____

_____

_____

*Continued on the next page.*

Think of someone with whom you work easily and encounter little to no resistance. You trust them and your communication with that person is effortless. Who is that person?

_____

What is it about that person and how you relate to him or her that comes naturally and positively?

_____

_____

_____

_____

_____

Study and perhaps model that person and their style of communicating. What skills do they have that you could use to strengthen your civility muscles?

_____

_____

_____

_____

Do you approach that person differently? Do you have a different attitude with them? When you leave his or her presence, do you feel different? If so, how?

_____

_____

_____

_____

_____

Do your core values come into play regularly in that relationship? If so, how?

_____

_____

_____

_____

_____

Communicating Character by Exercising Civility

## STRENGTHENING YOUR CHARACTER

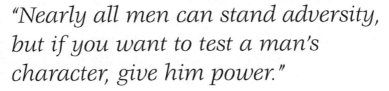

*"Nearly all men can stand adversity, but if you want to test a man's character, give him power."*

—Abraham Lincoln

Quick! Think of an individual who you consider the epitome of someone with a strong character. What is it about that person that makes you think of him or her as an example of character? Do the qualities of integrity, confidence, honesty, courage, and civility come to mind? People with strong character treat others with respect.

Consider specific examples of how they show respect, even amidst confrontation, disagreement, or debate. Describe those examples.

_____

_____

_____

_____

_____

With those qualities in mind, consider what you could incorporate in your interactions with others to demonstrate that strength of character. Remember: You **Communicate** your **Character** by how you exercise your **Civility**. Your character is reflected by your civility.

_____

_____

_____

_____

_____

Are your emotions getting in the way of the power of your civility? In chapter 12 of _Civility Unleashed_, I refer to the wisdom of the most successful and perhaps influential coach in the history of college basketball, John Wooden. Coach Wooden was uncompromising when it came to emotionalism—he did not tolerate extremes of positive and negative emotions and that was a big part of his success. What emotions are weakening your ability to handle a rude customer, insubordinate direct report, or condescending leader?

_____

_____

_____

_____

_____

What steps can you take to regain control and your ability to respond with civility?

_____

_____

_____

_____

# C's the Day EXERCISE

Please consider again the person you regard as the epitome of an individual of strong character. What do you think his/her core values include?

_____

_____

_____

Consider the specific ways that he or she expresses those core values toward others and themselves.

_____

_____

_____

**Communicating Character by Exercising Civility**

## EMOTIONALISM: THE ENEMY OF BUILDING STRENGTH

> *"Emotionalism—ups and downs in moods, displays of temperament—is almost always counterproductive, and at times disastrous."*
>
> — John Wooden

One of your greatest deterrents to building strong civility muscles is **emotionalism**. Coach Wooden defined emotionalism as ups and down in moods—think moodiness. He said, "...my strong belief that consistency, steadiness, and dependability are necessary for high-performance results and for Competitive Greatness. And emotionalism destroys all of this."[1]

Do you consider yourself a moody person? Are you up one moment, down the next? Do you walk into work smiling and greeting everyone with a "good morning," and the next day don't even make eye contact as you rush to your office? If any of this sounds familiar, I'll let you in on something: no one knows what to expect from you—and I promise, they're walking on eggshells or avoiding you. I'm not saying that all emotions are bad. It's emotionalism—striking out at others with the negative emotions of anger and hostility—that is harmful. Emotionalism also can be striking out at yourself with fear, self-condemnation, or self-loathing, and maybe even sadness. Those negative emotions don't put you into a position of strength to handle whatever resistance or obstacle is thrown at you. They do the opposite. Being self-aware is key to strong and flexible civility muscles. When you know yourself, you know your triggers and you know your moods.

What steps can **you** take to ensure that you are in control of your negative emotions and they're not in control of you? Consider these possibilities:

- Better prepare for the task at hand
- Take a deep breath before engaging
- Make self-control a top priority
- Understand that others are watching, listening, and being influenced—by you!
- Realize that you are creating a habit
- Ask yourself: Is this my strongest civil self?
- If my core value is _____ (fill in the blank), does my behavior display that value?

### Tackling Emotionalism Step-by-Step

Consider the last couple of times your tongue responded faster than your brain. Keeping those experiences in mind, please answer the following questions:

What happened that provoked your negative emotional response?

_____

_____

_____

_____

_____

Do these incidents involve the same person(s)? If so, who?

_____

_____

_____

What is it about that specific interaction that prompts your response?

_____

_____

_____

_____

_____

Identify your feelings at the time of the incident (sadness, fear, anger, threat).

_____

_____

_____

_____

_____

# C's the Day EXERCISE

Now you've identified contributing factors. You're not in the dark about what's happening. You know how you respond rubs off on those around you. With this clarity, create a game plan for the next time you're in a similar situation.

You probably won't master these interactions overnight. The next time you are in a similar position, record specifics.

What worked well?

_____

_____

_____

_____

_____

What didn't work well?

_____

_____

_____

_____

_____

Identify at least one specific step you could change (your attitude, your verbal response, your body language, what "facts" you're telling yourself at the moment, your "take-aways" from the exchange). What else can you change and how?

_____

_____

_____

_____

_____

**Communicating Character by Exercising Civility**

# C's the Day EXERCISE

Pause and consider your core values—those that you wrote down earlier. Write how those core values do or do not align with emotionalism.

_____

_____

_____

_____

_____

**Communicating Character by Exercising Civility**

Okay! Let's do some lifting!

## TIME TO DO SOME HEAVY LIFTING

*"Courage is resistance to fear, mastery of fear, not absence of fear."*

—Mark Twain

Let's walk through some scenarios—consider them your heavy lifting. How would you react in the following situations? What can you do to put yourself into the position of strength?

You've just earned a promotion. Rather than being a peer, you're now the boss. You know that the environment is toxic—there's a lot of gossip, undermining, belittling, and finger pointing. At least before, you could complain along with everyone else. Now, you realize it's up to you to do something about it. What are some steps you could take to be in a stronger position and to be an influence for civility?

1. Give up, and let your superior fix it.

2. Continue along as before, and just joke about the ugly situation.

3. Begin the process of defining the culture of trust, using the language of civility to get there.

Choice number three is the clear winner here. What specific steps can you take to begin the process?

_____

_____

_____

_____

_____

You're a leader with a team that's doing well, but you're aware of some friction among team members. The friction not only is among the members of the team, but between one or two of the members and you as well. What can you do?

1. The team works pretty well now, why bother doing anything? It will only rock the boat.

2. Determine whether your team subscribes to the defined culture of trust. If not, why? If so, is there one person who's eating away at the trust? How? Why? How can you get them on board?

3. Allow the team to define the person or persons who don't have full "buy-in" and let them handle it on their own.

If you selected the second choice, determine what steps you can take. You might begin by defining the culture of trust. Is everyone on board with it? Why or why not? Keep going in this direction.

_____

_____

_____

_____

_____

You're stuck in a toxic environment. You may even be the person with a target on your back. Your boss (or a person of influence) has made it very clear that you are no longer welcome in this workplace. You can't quit—you need the paycheck. What steps can you take to keep yourself healthy emotionally, mentally, and physically?

1. You realize you're a target. That's obvious. You've made the decision, however, to remain strong. You're going to look confident, communicate respectfully, and be sure that what you're communicating to yourself puts you in a position of strength—you're the victor, not the victim.

2. See yourself as the victim. After all, you are. Keep your head down and plow ahead. You're losing sleep, eating poorly, and dragging that negativity home with you.

3. Get angry. You know you're a victim. Undermine everyone who's out to get you, gossip, and try to generate as much drama as possible.

If you chose number one (phew! Everyone, including you, will be in a much better place emotionally!), what specific steps will you take to maintain your position of strength? Revisit chapter 13 in *Civility Unleashed* if you need reminders.

_____

_____

_____

_____

_____

# C's the Day EXERCISE

It's core value time! Review your choices and the steps you wrote, keeping your core values in mind. Do your actions reflect your core values?

If yes, terrific! If not, how can you make some changes that align your actions and core values?

_____

_____

_____

_____

_____

**Communicating Character by Exercising Civility**

## NOTES PART I

[1]   John Wooden and Steve Jamison, *Wooden on Leadership* (New York: McGraw-Hill, 2005), p. 113.

# PART II: CARDIO

# MOVING FROM STRENGTH-TRAINING TO CARDIO

 *"Wherever you go, go with all your heart."*

—Confucius

Well done! You've begun the ongoing work to grow your civility muscles. You've set goals for increasing your strength, identifying your core values, and regularly assessing your progress. You've even identified sources of resistance—by others and within yourself. You've begun to regard resistance and obstacles as a means of growth rather than failure.

Now, let's put down the weights and move onto your heart with some cardio exercises!

### Leading with Your Heart

To be healthy, you need to be strong. You need to be flexible. You also need a healthy heart.

If your heart gives out, you're in trouble—big trouble. Yet all too often, we expect our hearts to keep pumping no matter how much we ignore them.

Most of us figure our tickers will just keep ticking. Too often, our idea of exercising is to jump—into a pile of junk food. Brownies beat broccoli, surfing the net trumps a run through the neighborhood, and one more beer sounds so much better than one more glass of water! (For this Southern-born girl, it's iced tea loaded with sugar.)

It's much the same in our professional lives. We take for granted that our workplaces will chug along and maintain pace with the competition even if we ignore what's happening inside. We assume that employees and customers know that we appreciate them and their contributions. We figure that it's the mental piece, not the heart piece, that's critical in achieving remarkable results. However, you can't ignore the heartbeat of your workplace and then be surprised when there's turnover, turmoil, and trouble. The heart of any workplace needs the right kind of activity and the right kind of ingredients to nurture it.

### Your Goal

Again, it's time to pause. Please take a moment to think about why you're focusing on your heart and the role it plays in your workplace. Exactly what is your goal?

_____

_____

_____

_____

Do you want to learn to connect with your colleagues? Is your goal to begin to understand why you and others on your team don't see eye-to-eye? Is your goal to elicit a smile on your client's face the way your colleague can? Is your goal to leave at the end of the day feeling that you've made a positive difference in someone's life? What is your goal? Do you have more than one? Please write them here. If you've written more than one, please prioritize your goals. At the very least, prioritize your number 1 goal.

_____

_____

_____

_____

Terrific! Now place your written number 1 goal in prominent places—near your computer screen, on your mirror, on your phone, on your coffee cup, on your treadmill handle! Every time you see your goal, think about it. It will remind you of why you're working to make the changes you are.

Grab your water bottle—you're about to get that heart of yours beating!

## START MY BEATING HEART!

■ *"A loving heart is the truest wisdom."*

—Charles Dickens

You're surrounded by treadmills, stair-steppers, and elliptical bikes. Or perhaps you're trying to follow the steps of your instructor in an aerobics class like Zumba. Whether you're on a machine or in a class, the goal is the same: get your heart pumping to improve your circulatory system and boost your endurance! This is the part of *The Civility Workout* that I like to compare to the cardio portion of a fitness plan. This is where you really sweat!

Although many of us look at cardio exercise as a way to burn calories, it has many other benefits as well. It prevents stress, promotes focus, interrupts anxiety, regulates depression, promotes brain growth, and reduces belly fat.[1] On my best days when I've focused on exercising heart-based civility—really worked to understand the other person's viewpoint, to show consideration for them—I can tell you it has indeed helped reduce and prevent stress, prompted a joyful feeling, deterred anxiety, and demanded that I focus on others' wants and needs as well as my own. However, I've got to tell you, it's never done a thing for that jiggly stuff around my waist!

The benefits of your cardio workout in the civility gym have many of the same benefits as your cardio workout for fitness. It helps prevent stress—not only for you, but for others as well. It can induce a joyful feeling and deter anxiety. It requires endurance for you to stick with your new goals and behaviors. And it definitely demands that you focus on the wants and needs of someone else as well as your own.

Those benefits, however, don't come without work! The cardio piece of *The Civility Workout* makes its demands on your heart. It requires you to look at a situation from another person's point of view, and it calls on you to be empathetic and respond with kindness when it would be easier to react with anger. And let's not forget that a big part of the heart is passion.

Before proceeding though, pause, pull out a pen, and assess your heart-fueled civility. Are you ready to run full-speed up the hills of San Francisco or slowly amble to the nearest corner of your block?

## CIVILITY QUOTIENT ASSESSMENT—CARDIO

Again, it's a 1 to 5 scoring. Please circle 1 if you feel your heart plays no part in your relating to any of the statements listed below. Circle 5 if you feel you're guided by heart-felt constructive and positive emotions in the description. Of the 18 questions, there's the potential for a low score of 18 and a high score of 90.

| | | | | | |
|---|---|---|---|---|---|
| I try to understand the other person's perspective. | 1 | 2 | 3 | 4 | 5 |
| I'm patient when giving instructions. | 1 | 2 | 3 | 4 | 5 |
| I do not gossip. | 1 | 2 | 3 | 4 | 5 |
| I show appreciation to the people with whom I work and my customers. | 1 | 2 | 3 | 4 | 5 |
| I don't give feedback with the intention to hurt or embarrass. | 1 | 2 | 3 | 4 | 5 |
| I'm upbeat and positive when I first enter the workplace for the day. | 1 | 2 | 3 | 4 | 5 |
| I never reprimand someone publicly. | 1 | 2 | 3 | 4 | 5 |
| I give the benefit of the doubt to others. | 1 | 2 | 3 | 4 | 5 |
| I listen with the intention to understand the speaker. | 1 | 2 | 3 | 4 | 5 |
| I don't interrupt my direct reports when they're speaking. | 1 | 2 | 3 | 4 | 5 |
| I never roll my eyes in a meeting at someone's suggestions. | 1 | 2 | 3 | 4 | 5 |
| I am passionate about what I do. | 1 | 2 | 3 | 4 | 5 |
| I don't let others' negativity drag me down. | 1 | 2 | 3 | 4 | 5 |
| I tell the truth. | 1 | 2 | 3 | 4 | 5 |
| I try to be sincerely kind and respectful— not artificially sweet. | 1 | 2 | 3 | 4 | 5 |
| I trust the people with whom I work to do the right thing. | 1 | 2 | 3 | 4 | 5 |
| I can handle feedback (even if it's negative). I'll learn something from it. | 1 | 2 | 3 | 4 | 5 |
| I admit when I make a mistake. | 1 | 2 | 3 | 4 | 5 |

## *Scoring*

How did you do? Again, an assessment is not to be used one time only. The Civility Quotient Assessments are for you to use repeatedly to track your progress. Are you improving, sliding back into familiar and unhealthy habits, or stuck?

If you're going through *The Civility Workout* with another person, you may want to review the assessment with him or her. You just may find that their perspective is not only helpful, but that they provide needed insight.

## ARE YOU AT YOUR TARGET HEARTRATE?

Now that you've taken this assessment, review your scores. Do they indicate your heart plays a big part in your interactions and communications throughout the day? This is neither about everyone sitting around in a big hug-fest, nor is this about everyone agreeing on all decisions. This is about treating others (and yourself) with respect, kindness, and courtesy.

It's your heart that sparks your empathy, understanding, even courage on behalf of others. It's your heart that ignites your kindness, courtesy, and appreciation. It's your heart that lights up with encouragement, cheerfulness, and joy. Your heart is essential to pumping your life blood through your body; in much the same way, your heart pumps life into every one of your interactions and relationships. Start to pay attention to see the connection between your heart and your action or inactions. Sometimes your heart warns you that it's not necessary to have the last word! It is your heart that builds connections. And it's your heart that goes to work to listen without jumping to conclusions.

If your Civility Quotient Assessment—Cardio is loaded with 5s, consider the power of you! Could you help mentor or coach someone who is struggling in this area? Understand that if you're modeling heart-based behaviors, you are influencing others. You just may be what's urgently needed in a toxic environment.

If your assessment is loaded with circled 1s and 2s, consider chipping away at the wall around your heart. It could be that you've never been around people who are kind, supportive, and nonjudgmental. You don't even know what hanging around that type of person looks like, sounds like, or feels like. If that's the case, it's time to find some people who uplift you—even if they're not at work. It's important to be around people who exude caring about others. Moods and behaviors are contagious—you just might need to "catch" some behavior that is heart-centered.

If your assessment is filled with 3s and 4s, you're getting there but you've still got some work to do. Jump in and get to it right now. We need you! We all need your power of influence. Remember that we're facing a crisis of trust, and where there's no trust, there's no civility. We need your power of influence to welcome civility into your work arena.

After looking at your scores, please fill in the blanks.

List all the areas where you scored yourself 1s and 2s. These are the areas on which you need to focus.

_____

_____

_____

_____

_____

Now list the areas where you scored 4s and 5s. These strong points help you generate trust.

_____

_____

_____

_____

_____

Identify why it's hard for you to exercise a heart-centered approach with other people. Does it feel phony? Is it that you don't know **how** to let your heart take the lead? Are you afraid that you'll look soft? Did someone take advantage of you, and now you struggle with trust? Is there one person that prompts the stakes to go up around your heart? Is it working with a specific team, leader, or department that cues you to shut down your spark of kindness and courtesy?

_____

_____

_____

_____

_____

# C's the Day EXERCISE

Please review your Civility Quotient Assessment—Cardio. Are your responses and your core values aligned? If not, why not?

The fact is that we all, at times, behave in a way that isn't in alignment with our core values. That's why this is an ongoing exercise. Remember, you're working to create habits that lead to your civil self.

**Communicating Character by Exercising Civility**

Next up—what happens to you when your civil self becomes more heart-centered!

## PUT YOUR HEART INTO IT!

 *"Friends show their love in times of trouble, not in happiness."*

—Euripides

If you've ever worked out and your trainer yelled, "Come on, put your heart into it!" you know what she meant. Crank it up. Work harder. Stick with it and don't quit! Put all your energy into it!

If you were to put more heart into it in the workplace, how would you crank it up? Here's what will happen to you as you put more energy into exercising heart-centered civility. You will be more:

- ☐ Empathetic
- ☐ Effective at listening
- ☐ Kind
- ☐ Collaborative
- ☐ Focused on team results
- ☐ Accountable
- ☐ Team focused
- ☐ Supportive
- ☐ Encouraging
- ☐ Aware
- ☐ Committed to be a positive influence
- ☐ Fun
- ☐ Loyal

- ☐ Dependable
- ☐ Engaged in your work and in your professional relationships
- ☐ Committed
- ☐ Willing to share credit
- ☐ Humble
- ☐ Trusting
- ☐ Trustworthy
- ☐ Focused on outstanding results
- ☐ Enthusiastic
- ☐ Energetic
- ☐ Positive

# C's the Day EXERCISE

Review the list above and check **three words** that best describe the areas where you would like to improve yourself. Think about it this way: These are the words you want people in your professional life (and/or personal life) to use when they **describe you**! These are the three words that you want to align with.

Now, for each word, write **three clear-cut steps** you can take to make improvements.

_____

_____

_____

_____

_____

**Communicating Character by Exercising Civility**

You can approach this **C's the Day EXERCISE** by thinking of a specific person or situation that challenges your efforts to be civil.

For instance, you may have checked **effective at listening**. Specifically, you want to improve your listening skills with your colleague, Jennifer. You tend to interrupt Jennifer and check your email when she comes to you for advice. You always assume you know where Jennifer's going in the conversation.

Your three specific steps may be:

1. Stop interrupting! Be conscious about waiting until Jennifer finishes speaking before you begin speaking.

2. Look at Jennifer, not at your computer or phone.

3. Ask questions to be sure you understand Jennifer's point.

Or you can be more general in your goals. For example, you want to improve your listening skills with your peers, leaders, direct reports, and customers. You know you tend to interrupt and show impatience when someone else is speaking.

Your three steps are:

1. Take a breath, be conscious of not jumping in.

2. Maintain appropriate eye-contact.

3. Listen to understand the other person's concern—and again, breathe.

Okay, now it's your turn! From the checklist on page 34, write your top three items.

Descriptive word #1: _____

Three steps for improvement:

_____

_____

_____


Descriptive word #2: _____

Three steps for improvement:

_____

_____

_____


Descriptive word #3: _____

Three steps for improvement:

_____

_____

_____

If you're trying to increase your endurance through your cardio exercise, please understand it won't happen overnight. You're not going to jog around the block today and tomorrow run a marathon. It takes ongoing effort with incremental improvements. I used to jog six miles every morning. I began by running around a couple of blocks. That was it! I couldn't even imagine running a mile. Little by little, step by step, block by block, I reached a daily goal of six miles. If I'd tried to run a couple of miles the first day, I would have injured myself and created my own setbacks.

Exercising civility consistently doesn't happen overnight either. Little by little you learn what works, and maybe even more importantly, what doesn't! Niceness to the point of sickeningly sweet will undermine your efforts and your results. It's overkill. You'll harm the relationship because it's not genuine. Be patient with yourself. You are developing your civil self!

This brings me to finding a companion on this expedition. When I ran those six miles, I ran with a friend. We talked, laughed, and had great conversations. If I hadn't had a running partner, it would have been more difficult and no fun!

Consider enlisting the help of a colleague whom you trust to give you suggestions, feedback, and even a bit of cheerleading along the way. We all can use a pat on the back in the civility gym.

### Keep at It!

We all know that creating a culture of trust is invaluable! When you work in a culture of trust, you look forward to spending time with your colleagues. So then, what the heck gets in the way?

That's next, so don't slow down!

## TRIGGERS AND HOT BUTTONS: THE ENEMY OF THE HEART

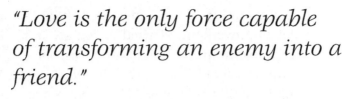

*"Love is the only force capable of transforming an enemy into a friend."*

—Martin Luther King, Jr.

In chapter 3 of *Civility Unleashed*, I focus on "Incivility: The Dark Side of Bad Behavior." Some of the greatest instigators of rotten behavior are our own triggers and hot buttons.

**Something** or **someone** sets us off. We react! We don't respond with a smidgen of thought behind our actions—we have an immediate or knee-jerk reaction with little or no consideration for consequences. And our knees aren't the only jerks at times like these.

We usually blame the "trigger" or "hot button." It's **their** fault that we respond in a snippy way. If they hadn't aggravated us, we would have responded to their email in a timely manner. And it's certainly not our fault for walking around with chips on our shoulders and looks of disgust on our faces.

It's as though we have no control over ourselves! The fact is we hand over our control to other people when we behave poorly and reactively. We've put "them" in our driver's seat. I know what that feels like—in a toxic environment, that's exactly what I did all too many times. I gave away my control.

A **trigger** is defined as "anything, as an act or event that serves as a stimulus and initiates or precipitates a reaction or series of reactions."[2] In non-dictionary language and for our purposes, a trigger is something that sparks incivility. Although a trigger is something that would produce a reaction in most of us (such as a colleague who constantly interrupts you), a **hot button** is specific to an individual. One of my hot buttons is the person who shows up late to work with an expensive cup of coffee in his hand. Getting coffee was the priority, not getting to work on time.

Triggers can include:

- That morning person who's loud and really happy from the moment they walk in the door
- The non-morning person who grumbles as they walk through the office and never responds to your "good morning"
- The person who never responds to your emails without your prodding
- The person who prods you about responding to his or her emails
- The person who never says "please" or "thank you"
- The person who wants you to walk through every detail
- The person who doesn't explain in detail
- The person who asks you about your diet
- The person who never comments on your weight loss
- Postings on social media
- Public reprimands

Hot buttons can include:

- The person whose desk is always a disaster when you need to locate something on it
- The person who looks over your shoulder to see what's on your computer screen
- Political conversations
- Religious conversations
- Conversations about someone's health
- Explaining again—and again—and again
- Borrowing your favorite pen—and never returning it
- Asking for a favor—at the last minute
- The whiner
- The drama queen or king
- The gossip
- The person who wears sickeningly sweet or too much perfume

# C's the Day EXERCISE

What are your triggers and hot buttons? Being aware of them gives you the opportunity to take control of them rather than letting your triggers and hot buttons snatch control from you. Make a list. Then determine which triggers and hot buttons on your list get to you fastest and hit you the hardest.

_____

_____

_____

_____

_____

**Communicating Character by Exercising Civility**

For example, you've explained the same steps in a system to Hank over and over and over again. And yet, Hank keeps returning to run through them "one more time." You've increasingly responded to Hank with a heavy sigh, (almost) a roll of your eyes, and exasperation in your voice. But now, you're thinking with your "heart." As you see Hank approach, you think about "connecting" with him rather than getting him on his way as quickly as possible. You greet him with a smile, and ask him where the problem seems to lie. You evaluate whether you are explaining too quickly, leaving out steps, explaining orally when Hank's a visual learner, or is your impatient behavior prompting Hank to shut down his own learning process? Your approach is completely different this time. Does this guarantee that Hank won't be back again with the same question? No, but you're beginning to truly listen, understand, and connect.

# C's the Day EXERCISE

What steps can you take to minimize the effect of that trigger or hot button? Remember, we're focusing on the heart!

_____

_____

_____

_____

_____

**Communicating Character by Exercising Civility**

# C's the Day EXERCISE

Return to your list of three core values. Determine how your triggers and hot buttons affect how you align yourself with your core values. I bet they create a wedge in that alignment. How can your core values reduce the "control" of your triggers and hot buttons?

_____

_____

_____

_____

_____

**Communicating Character by Exercising Civility**

Imagine your strong and heart-centered civil self. Now, imagine the gifts that your civil self could bring to the workplace. Stop imagining—and do it. That's next!

## GIFTS FROM YOUR HEART

 *"The deepest principle of human nature is the craving to be appreciated."*

—William James

I want you to pause, take a deep breath, and think about how far you've come. You've identified three core values that you are using to measure and guide your communication and behavior—your civility.

You've identified areas of resistance that used to block your progress in connecting with others. Now, you're building endurance—so much, in fact, that hurdles now are a welcome opportunity to demonstrate your ability to exercise civility under stress. You've looked for models of character, and you now model character. You're poised and in control of your emotions. You've also identified your triggers and hot buttons.

And now it's time for you to identify the specific gifts that you can give freely and frequently. Remember, your goal here is to become your civil self who helps create and maintain a culture of trust. When you grow trust, you grow relationships that are solid, proven, and steadfast. You are connecting.

The two gifts that will maximize those connections are a smile and appreciation. Mother Teresa wisely told us, "Peace begins with a smile—smile five times a day at someone you don't really want to smile at. Do it for peace."

Imagine peace in your workplace! Less drama, even **no** drama, and that vacuum filled with peace. If peace begins with a smile, let it begin with you.

# C's the Day EXERCISE

Think of someone or several people with whom you struggle. Smiling at them is beyond challenging for you. So just do it. Write that individual's name, or better yet—come up with some fun name for them to ensure privacy, and remember to be civil when you do it (snark has no place in a civil environment!). Now smile at them five times a day. Chart your progress for each time you smiled at them!

Code Name                                              Times You Smiled

_____  ☐  ☐  ☐  ☐  ☐

_____  ☐  ☐  ☐  ☐  ☐

_____  ☐  ☐  ☐  ☐  ☐

_____  ☐  ☐  ☐  ☐  ☐

_____  ☐  ☐  ☐  ☐  ☐

**Communicating Character by Exercising Civility**

# C's the Day EXERCISE

What are your obstacles to smiling? Please write them here (for example, it feels fake, you think you have an ugly smile, no one ever smiles back, etc.).

_____

_____

_____

**Communicating Character by Exercising Civility**

If you're still struggling to smile, consider this: genuinely smiling releases hormones that contribute to our feeling happy. A smile makes you look younger. And smiles are contagious!

### Show Appreciation

There's nothing more heart-centered and will expedite connections better than honest and sincere appreciation. Appreciation demands **awareness** and **humility**.

- **Awareness.** Pay attention to what people are doing and how their efforts bring positive consequences.

- **Humility.** Give credit to others. Don't expect to receive it. Give it away!

# C's the Day EXERCISE

Write the steps you'll take to show appreciation. Who deserves appreciation? From whose work have you benefited? Who's had a great idea? Who is becoming a better leader and/or contributor to your workplace? Who makes your time in the office better? More fun? More productive? More positive?

_____

_____

_____

_____

_____

Not everyone finds it easy to show appreciation. What about you? Is it easy or difficult? When it's difficult, is it because of the person involved or the situation? Identify why appreciation is difficult.

_____

_____

_____

Now identify three steps you can take to show appreciation where you aren't now.

_____

_____

_____

**Communicating Character by Exercising Civility**

# C's the Day EXERCISE

Pause and consider how your three core values help you to initiate smiling and appreciation.

_____

_____

_____

_____

_____

**Communicating Character by Exercising Civility**

Is there someone in your worplace who has the power to motivate? Let's study that person next.

## STRENGTH OF HEART

Quick! Think of someone who you consider an example of someone who motivates others. As if by magic, this person touches others in a way that sparks the recipient's passion, engagement, and revs their heart. What qualities come to mind when you consider that individual? Perhaps the qualities include kindness, enthusiasm, joy, excitement, compassion, clarity, energy, empathy, patience, and humility. Maybe what touches your heart is that you know they have your back! Please write those qualities below.

_____

_____

_____

You've identified specific qualities of your heart-centered motivator. (Please don't think that this is a person who oozes sweetness. This is an individual who connects!) Now think about a specific incident in which you saw the person you identified above exhibit those qualities. Please write which qualities they exhibited and what was remarkable about that scenario. Don't forget to include how they used that specific quality.

_____

_____

_____

Which of those qualities could you include in your day-to-day interactions that would strengthen how you influence your culture toward civility?

_____

_____

_____

Return to chapter 9 of *Civility Unleashed* for the example of Coach Mike Krzyzewski's deep appreciation for teamwork. Keeping in mind Coach K's description of five players working as one, please answer these questions: Do you regularly show empathy toward your colleagues and direct reports (and even your leaders)? If not, what's getting in the way? Could it be that you don't understand the values of working as a team?

_____

_____

_____

Sometimes when you have a goal in mind when it comes to fitness, you'll have a setback. We all do. There's an injury, a vacation, extra demands at work—something gets in the way of your progress toward the goal. That can certainly happen with your civility training as well. If you've had setbacks, what specific steps can you now take to regain control of your civility?

_____

_____

_____

Outstanding! I'm so proud of you. It's hard work to embrace introspection, self-examination, and an ongoing exercise of the elements of civility!

---

# C's the Day EXERCISE

It's core values time. If you've had a setback and are struggling to regain control of your civil self, how can you use your core values to help you re-set and re-start?

_____

_____

_____

**Communicating Character by Exercising Civility**

---

So, let's see what happens if we crank it up a bit!

## TIME TO GO FOR IT!

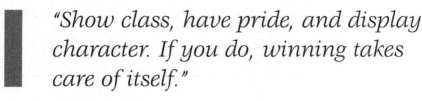

*"Show class, have pride, and display character. If you do, winning takes care of itself."*

—Paul Bryant

Let's run through some scenarios. Think of them as running the hills of San Francisco. How would you react? What can you do to navigate with heart?

You have a direct report with whom you struggle. He's excellent in exceeding his sales quota. However, back in the office, he makes life difficult for his peers and support staff. He's arrogant, demanding, and rude. Your boss doesn't want you to fire him because of his effect on the bottom line. What are some steps that you can take to try to eliminate his negativity and its fallout in your workplace?

1.  Make life miserable for him so that he quits on his own.

2.  Allow him to continue to berate those with whom he works.

3.  Sit down with him and clearly define your expectations for a culture of trust for your workplace and his accountability to it. You know that you may also need to sit down with your boss and show the financial impact on the turnover, lack of engagement, disloyalty, gossip, and negativity that is exhibited by members of your team who are regularly subjected to his rudeness.

If you chose number 3 (I know number 1 is very tempting, but you can't go there!), how would you proceed?

You're a leader who inherited a team that's had a very unpleasant history together. They gossip about one another, undermine each other, and disrespect each other constantly. You can't wish them away and you can't fire them in the immediate future. What do you do?

1.  Give up and let them continue to bicker—that's all they know.

2. Call a meeting and demand that they behave like grownups.

3. Call a meeting and describe the expected culture of trust. Ask for your team's input. What do they see as obstacles? What are smoother paths to get there?

You're stuck in a toxic environment. Perhaps you're the target. Using your heart-centered civil self, how can you proceed to protect yourself and put yourself in a positon to wrestle back control of your day?

1. You know you're a victim, you see yourself as a victim, and you behave like a victim.

2. You take a hard look at the situation and see that you are performing above expectations. You decide to **C's the Day** and take control of yourself physically, mentally, and emotionally. You eat with your health in mind, exercise whether you want to or not, and create a regular routine for sleep. You adjust your viewing and listening habits of videos, music, podcasts, and TV to ensure what you're watching is feeding you positively. You walk into the office with your head held high. And you have great respect for your civil self.

3. You shut down. You don't interact with your colleagues, avoid your offenders, and do the minimum job you can.

If you chose number 2, congratulations. When I was in a toxic environment, that is not what I did, and I learned by experience that had I changed my diet and exercise, I would have been in a far stronger position. I needed to eat three nutritious meals a day and get my blood flowing with physical exercise no matter how little time or energy I had. Learn from my mistake! What other specific steps would you take?

_____

_____

_____

_____

_____

# C's the Day EXERCISE

Core value time! Review both your choices and follow-up steps and their alignment or misalignment with your core values. What did you learn from this exercise?

_____

_____

_____

_____

_____

**Communicating Character by Exercising Civility**

## NOTES PART II

[1] Misato Alexandre, _5 Incredible Health Benefits of Regular Cardio Exercises_, Fitwrr, available at http://www.fitwirr.com/fitness/-5-health-benefits-regular-cardio-exercise.

[2] Dictionary.com, s.v. "trigger."

# PART III: FLEXIBILITY

# MOVING FROM CARDIO TO FLEXIBILITY

■ *"Flexibility is the key to stability."*

—John Wooden

Congratulations! You've given your heart a workout! I know you've built endurance and are more empathetic and better able to connect. Your heart-centered civil approach and your powerful civil musculature have combined to develop you into an individual who is accountable, holds others accountable, and can understand another's perspective.

Now, you can step down from your fast pace for a bit, take a deep breath, and prepare to focus on flexibility. Think of it as stepping into a yoga class.

## Influencing through Flexibility

Look at the pros in just about any sport and you'll find that they not only work out to build strength and cardio endurance, but they also work on their flexibility—both physical and mental. They not only have to adapt to the changing course of a ball, unexpected moves by their opponents, changing conditions in the weather, but they must also adjust for a change in game plan by the coach. Failure to adjust would result in, well—failure!

Every day is game day in our workplaces. We think we know the game plan—and then look!—there's a change by leadership. We've been told our budget is set, and then it gets cut. We've come to trust our team, and then someone moves or worse, destroys our trust.

Communication styles differ, personalities vary, and what was respectfully accepted yesterday, is disrespectfully denied today.

If you're unable to bend, stretch, and be resilient, you're in trouble. So again, breathe deeply and let's begin.

## *Your Goal*

I want you to start thinking about when it would have paid to have been flexible. What about that meeting when you refused to back down from your opinion of what to do and how to do it? Or what about that time when you refused to see that there was another way to accomplish the same task? How about when you had the ability to bounce back from a very negative encounter with your leadership at that particularly volatile team meeting? Determine your goal(s) for this next section. Consider what the qualities of flexibility and resiliency would mean for you.

_____

_____

_____

Pick your top goal. Write it here and write it in various areas where you can see it: on your yoga mat, on the refrigerator, or even as a pop-up text on your phone.

_____

_____

_____

OK, you're about to get started. Time to take yet another deep breath!

## STRETCH WHO YOU ARE

> *"Those who cannot change their minds cannot change anything."*
>
> —George Bernard Shaw

Flexibility brings with it beauty, balance, and the opportunity to stretch every inch of yourself. You find yourself in positions that take you out of your comfort zone and into new and different stances. You expand your range of motion.

If you haven't spent much time stretching, bending, and working to increase flexibility, these activities may not seem athletic. But spend time with the pros, and you learn that working to increase your flexibility may improve your performance, decrease your risk of injuries, and enable your muscles to work more effectively.[1]

Step into a yoga or ballet class, and you'll stretch yourself into positions that are uncomfortable. Who knew that you could become a human pretzel! Each time you go further and hold a pose longer, you strengthen your body—and your mind. You build muscle memory and you build confidence.

There are no shortcuts. You do all the work yourself. And I promise you, it can be uncomfortable. You tell your body to move in a way it doesn't normally move, to breathe in a manner that you find unnatural, and to hold a weird and twisty position for what seems like eternity. The first time I tried yoga, it was in a class where it felt like they'd turned up the heat (oh wait, they had!). I was amazed at my flexibility—and how sore my muscles were the next day!

In the civility gym, flexibility plays an equally essential role. Far too many workplaces suffer injury and pain because of people's failure to yield. Intractable employees and leadership consider bending as failure. Workplaces suffer when they are rigid, uncompromising, and inflexible. Such an environment is the perfect breeding ground for incivility.

Working on flexibility in the civility gym demands patience, focus, attention, and even a little discomfort. After all, this is something new. Something different.

Before taking a deep breath and beginning our exercises, let's assess how flexible or inflexible you are.

## CIVILITY QUOTIENT ASSESSMENT–FLEXIBILITY

The scoring system remains the same. Please circle 1 if you feel that flexibility plays no part in your interactions in the workplace. Circle 5 if you feel that, like Elastigirl, you can be the hero of civility through your flexibility in the workplace. Of the 18 questions, there's the potential for a low score of 18 and a high score of 90.

| | | | | | |
|---|---|---|---|---|---|
| I handle change well. | 1 | 2 | 3 | 4 | 5 |
| I enjoy working with various individuals and teams. | 1 | 2 | 3 | 4 | 5 |
| I handle stress well. | 1 | 2 | 3 | 4 | 5 |
| I maintain a positive attitude even in a negative environment. | 1 | 2 | 3 | 4 | 5 |
| I bounce back well from confrontation. | 1 | 2 | 3 | 4 | 5 |
| I'm able to think clearly and behave well, even in chaos. | 1 | 2 | 3 | 4 | 5 |
| I don't consider myself rigid. | 1 | 2 | 3 | 4 | 5 |
| I'm inflexible about my core values, but not about how to demonstrate them. | 1 | 2 | 3 | 4 | 5 |
| When someone vigorously challenges me on my ideas, I bounce back. | 1 | 2 | 3 | 4 | 5 |
| I hold direct reports on my team accountable. | 1 | 2 | 3 | 4 | 5 |
| I hold the leadership on my team accountable. | 1 | 2 | 3 | 4 | 5 |
| I don't confuse flexibility with weakness. | 1 | 2 | 3 | 4 | 5 |
| I don't bend to everyone's wishes. | 1 | 2 | 3 | 4 | 5 |
| I remain flexible in the face of customers' complaints. | 1 | 2 | 3 | 4 | 5 |
| Being flexible doesn't mean standing for unethical behavior. | 1 | 2 | 3 | 4 | 5 |
| Taking a deep breath before responding has become second nature for me. | 1 | 2 | 3 | 4 | 5 |
| I am resilient. | 1 | 2 | 3 | 4 | 5 |
| I can consider other options even if I think my way is the best way. | 1 | 2 | 3 | 4 | 5 |

## Scoring

When you tally your score, how do you fare? Could you be teaching a yoga class in civility or would someone consider you as flexible as a flag pole? Remember, if you're going through this workbook with a Civility Workout partner, ask that person for their assessment of you. And then ask them why they graded you as they did. Remember, this is not about taking someone's numbers as criticism or a put down, this is feedback that helps you compare where you are now to where you want to be.

Be sure you thank your partner for his or her honesty. Telling someone something they may not want to hear is difficult. Your workout partner is trying to help you be your best civil self.

---

# C's the Day EXERCISE

Please review where you scored yourself 1s and 2s. Where should you put your focus? Are you flexible with some people, but not with others? Are you resilient when you've been knocked down? Do you hold some people accountable, but not others? List the areas you need to work on:

_____

_____

_____

_____

_____

*Continued on the next page.*

---

Now look at the areas where you scored yourself 4 or 5. How can you use those abilities to help your weaker areas?

_____

_____

_____

_____

_____

**Communicating Character by Exercising Civility**

# C's the Day EXERCISE

Are there certain topics/areas in which you are more inflexible (for example, tardiness and punctuality; asking for someone to cover for them at the last minute; orderliness of the office, desk, or vehicle; dress code compliance; follow-through; incivility in the workplace; cliques; gossip)?

_____

_____

_____

_____

Why do you think you're inflexible in these situations or with certain people?

_____

_____

_____

_____

What steps could you take to increase your resilience and/or flexibility in these situations?

_____

_____

_____

_____

_____

Does your rigidity or inflexibility get in the way of achieving your goals? How?

_____

_____

_____

_____

_____

Consider why it's difficult for you to be more flexible. Is it because you consider flexibility a weakness? Do you believe that if you "bend," you are no longer a person of principle? Do you see a difference between flexibility and being a pushover? Do you consider flexibility as adaptability? Has someone taken advantage of you when you were flexible? Has it happened frequently?

_____

_____

_____

_____

_____

*Continued on the next page.*

Are there certain circumstances under which you are more rigid? Do you find that your flexibility and inflexibility differ because of personal choices (for example, lack of sleep, getting to work late, eating poorly, etc.)? Are there certain individuals with whom you are more flexible or rigid?

_____

_____

_____

_____

**Communicating Character by Exercising Civility**

# C's the Day EXERCISE

Please review your Civility Quotient Assessment—Flexibility. Are your responses and core values aligned? Why or why not?

_____

_____

_____

_____

_____

**Communicating Character by Exercising Civility**

## PREPARATION

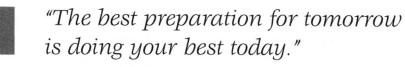

*"The best preparation for tomorrow is doing your best today."*

—H. Jackson Brown, Jr.

Flexibility in the workplace can mean a lot of different things today. It can mean flexibility in schedules—not the typical 9 to 5. It may describe a workplace that includes personal options of piercings, tattoos, and jeans. Heck, shoes are an option in many workplaces where everyone shuffles from office to office in socks or bare feet. It can mean an open office space that bears no resemblance to the conventional office of four walls, a door, and a great big desk. It may mean working on site or from home. Flexibility can refer to many exterior options.

But what we're talking about in the civility gym is your internal flexibility—the flexibility that resides within you. It's the ability to adapt to change, listen with a willingness to yield to another person's persuasion, and to share the floor, resources, and credit. Attentiveness to flexibility builds your civil self.

While empathy works the heart, flexibility works the mind. It demands your ability to look at the big picture and understand that for you to survive and thrive, you must make changes. Like a tennis player who adjusts to the trajectory and speed of the ball, you must have flexibility of reach, speed, and grit.

What qualities help you generate flexibility?

- **Preparation.** One of the best ways to stretch yourself for growth, change, and opportunity is to prepare yourself. How do you prepare yourself when you don't know what tomorrow will bring? Always do your best work and immerse yourself in ongoing learning. Be willing to say yes!

- **Confidence.** Stretch your confidence level by acting confident— even if you don't feel self-confident yet. Let others know that you're not stuck in a rut and are bold enough to try something that challenges you.

- **Network.** Find a mentor who's willing to help you stretch and prepare for change and growth. Listen for guidance, evaluation, and suggestions.

- **Observe.** Watch others as they adapt to change, confrontation, and challenges. You can also learn a lot from watching others not adapt to change, confrontation, and challenges.

- **Engage.** Don't sit back and stay stuck demanding that your way is the only way. Flexibility often leads to growth.

# C's the Day EXERCISE

**Preparation.** When you're prepared, you are in a better position to be flexible. What are you doing now to prepare yourself for opportunity and change? What do you commit to doing to prepare yourself for change and opportunity?

_____

_____

_____

_____

_____

**Confidence.** Even if you don't feel confident, you can build your confidence by creating opportunities to succeed. Athletes don't walk into their first game confident. They build confidence through practice and competition. Even if you fail, learning from an experience builds confidence. What specific steps are you taking to build your confidence?

_____

_____

_____

_____

_____

**Network.** Building a network of support allows you to be flexible. It's flexibility that builds the respectful behavior and communication with others. Support for that flexibility often comes from building a network of people who have your back and your ear. Ask questions and listen to their responses—and then be willing to challenge yourself. Who is in your network? What are your plans to build or expand your network?

_____

_____

_____

_____

_____

**Observe.** Sometimes it's hard to be flexible unless you've watched others stretch themselves and adapt to change with a positive attitude and confidence. Look inside and outside your organization for individuals who demonstrate their flexibility.

_____

_____

_____

_____

_____

*Continued on the next page.*

**Engage.** Now it's time to show others that you believe in a culture of trust. You can adapt to change, you are flexible, and your flexibility extends to your interactions with individuals. How can you engage? Are there opportunities in the future?

_____

_____

_____

_____

_____

**Communicating Character by Exercising Civility**

# C's the Day EXERCISE

Write below how becoming more flexible with others and with change aligns with your goals. Or do they?

_____

_____

_____

_____

Does your stretching yourself line up with your core values? How?

_____

_____

_____

_____

**Communicating Character by Exercising Civility**

## ENDLESS POSSIBILITIES

*"Nothing is impossible. The word itself says 'I'm possible.'"*

—Audrey Hepburn

Imagine if we took Audrey Hepburn's words to heart: "I'm possible." Our workplaces would overflow with cultures built on civility. Excuses would be on the way out, and possibilities for growth would be endless. Why? Because when optimism takes hold, civility does the same. Incivility, rudeness, and thoughtless behavior don't take root unless they're cultivated in the soil of fear, negativity, and anger.

As we develop our civil selves, one of the qualities we need to exercise regularly is resilience. Resilience is defined by the American Psychological Association as "the process of adapting well in the face of adversity, trauma, tragedy, threats or significant sources of stress."[2]

Although today's workplaces are filled with stress, what if they were also filled with resilience? It's resilience that allows you to exit a poor performance review and view it as a means for improvement rather than a reprimand. Imagine bouncing back from a dismal encounter with a supervisor and using that experience as a learning tool. It's resilience that empowers you to return to a meeting and learn the skills of assertiveness after times of condescension and rude behavior by others.

Which qualities best build resilience?

- **Humor.** I know, I know. The last thing you want to do when things go wrong is smile or laugh. Yet, it's that ability to discover something positive from the incident that allows you to bounce back.

- **Initiative.** As Jim Rohn said, "You need to stand up and do whatever is necessary to get back on course."

- **Instructive self-talk.** After an ugly encounter, a dismal failure, or a public reprimand, you need to ensure that the conversations you have in your head move you forward and upward, not backward and downward. Don't tear yourself down. This is the time to build your self-confidence and to move forward.

- **Defining yourself.** Don't define yourself by the negative occurrence.

- **Ask for advice.** Ask someone for their insight and guidance. This person doesn't have to be in your workplace. The person does need to be someone you trust!

---

# C's the Day EXERCISE

**Humor.** Consider the last time you had a setback, especially a major one that threw you for a loop. How could you have handled it with humor, or what could you do in the future to build resilience through humor?

_____

_____

_____

_____

_____

**Initiative.** Initiative brings with it creativity and imagination. Looking back, was there a way you could have taken initiative in a past experience that would have changed the outcome and your attitude? What could you do in the future?

_____

_____

_____

_____

_____

**Constructive self-talk.** What are the messages that are running rampant in your head? Are they negative or positive? How can you turn the negative messages into positive ones that are instructive and productive?

_____

_____

_____

_____

_____

**Defining yourself.** I want you to pause for a moment. Now consider this: are you defining yourself by your last unpleasant experience or exchange in the workplace? If so, flip it around. Change your narrative. Define yourself so that you put yourself in a position to empower you.

_____

_____

_____

_____

_____

**Ask for advice.** You wouldn't be embarrassed to ask a fitness instructor to show you the correct technique to perform a pushup. Don't hesitate to ask for advice or insight on how to handle setbacks from someone you admire. He or she is an individual of character, poise, and resilience. Who is on your list to contact?

_____

_____

_____

Communicating Character by Exercising Civility

# C's the Day EXERCISE

I want you to consider both your goal and your core values. How does this work bring you into greater alignment with those?

_____

_____

_____

_____

_____

**Communicating Character by Exercising Civility**

## STRETCHING WHAT'S WITHIN YOU

> *"My mission in life is not merely to survive, but to thrive; and to do so with some passion, some compassion, some humor, and some style."*
>
> —Maya Angelou

I want you to think of someone whom you've watched demonstrate flexibility to others. Okay? You have them in your thoughts. Now, think about how they show their willingness to break out of rigidity—whether it's their rigid opinions, behaviors, or way of doing things. Perhaps you've seen them try a new idea proposed by someone else. Maybe you've seen them adjust their communication to better connect with another person. Possibly, you've seen them abandon an old practice and replace it with a more efficient approach. You've seen them embrace change rather than fight or fear it. Write what you've witnessed, and what qualities you might embrace.

_____

_____

_____

_____

_____

From what you've witnessed, what steps could you take to be more flexible with others and to change with the challenges?

_____

_____

_____

_____

_____

What gets in the way of you being less rigid? If you're already flexible and adjust well to change, what actions do you take to maintain that approach?

_____

_____

_____

_____

_____

Think of someone who is resilient and write the qualities that make them so.

_____

_____

_____

_____

_____

If you consider yourself resilient, what do you do to develop and maintain that resiliency?

_____

_____

_____

_____

_____

If you do not consider yourself resilient, what steps could you take to develop resiliency?

_____

_____

_____

_____

_____

# C's the Day EXERCISE

Consider your core values. How could you embrace those values to help you become more flexible with change and with other people?

_____

_____

_____

_____

_____

How can your core values steer you toward greater resilience?

_____

_____

_____

_____

_____

**Communicating Character by Exercising Civility**

## YOUR TURN TO STRETCH

_"If you are lucky enough to be someone's employer, then you have a moral obligation to make sure people do look forward to coming to work in the morning."_

—John Mackey

Imagine that these scenes take place in your workplace. How would you stretch to produce positive results?

You've just received word that one of your favorite colleagues has been reassigned and is no longer part of your team. You trust this colleague (Jill) to produce top-quality results with no accompanying drama. Her replacement is a gentleman whom you only know by reputation—and his reputation is not good. Word is that he is undependable, rude, and likes to take credit for any success. How do you respond?

1.  Go to your supervisor immediately and demand that either Jill or someone with her experience and reputation be assigned back to your team. You're not about to stand for this nonsense.

2.  Say nothing and undermine the new guy. After all, you already know everything you need to know about him.

3.  Discuss, if possible, the changes so that you understand why the decision was made. Work with your team to embrace the changes. Be courteous to the new guy and give him the benefit of the doubt. Determine from your own experiences whether he's respectful and responsible.

What would that look like?

_____

_____

_____

_____

_____

You've been asked to take over a project that's behind schedule. It means using software that you're not very familiar with, and the deadline is coming up soon. You don't know the team well, and you already have a full plate. How do you stretch?

1.  Throw a temper tantrum so that you get everyone's attention—and perhaps their sympathy.

2. Return to your office and grumble about the unfairness of the situation. Make it very clear that the project will never come in on time—and you're not to blame.

3. Return to your office and analyze how you can handle the additional responsibilities. Take the time to reprioritize your previous and new responsibilities. Discuss with your boss, if possible, the changes. Delegate where you can. Ask IT to provide you with someone to give you a quick class on the challenging software. Begin strategizing to get buy-in and input from the current team to determine how to proceed.

Outline what steps you'd take to proceed to maintain a culture of trust and reach your goals.

_____

_____

_____

_____

_____

You were just raked over the coals by your boss in front of your own team in a meeting. You weren't given any opportunity to respond. You were caught entirely off-guard. And now you've been told that your neck is on the line if you don't make the sales numbers turn around—and fast. What do you do?

1. Get each of your team members aside and tell them how angry and embarrassed you are.

2. You return to your desk in a daze, and immediately sink into a deep funk.

3. You know that your boss has a point. Your numbers could be better. You also know that some of the best salespeople from the company recently retired and are a phone call away. You invite one or two of them out to lunch and ask for their advice. You also request a

meeting with your boss. Once together, you ask that your boss not reprimand you in a public setting.

If you map out the steps to take and redefine your self-talk, what would those look and sound like?

_____

_____

_____

_____

_____

## NOTES PART II

1   Mayo Clinic, "Stretching: Focus on Flexibility," available at http://www.mayoclinic.org/healthy-lifestyle/fitness/in-depth/stretching/art-20047931.

2   American Psychological Association, "The Road to Resilience," available at http://www.apa.org/helpcenter/road-resilience.aspx.

# PART IV: DIET

# THE CIVIL SELF DIET PLAN

■ *"The first wealth is health."*

—Ralph Waldo Emerson

Congratulations! I'm so proud of you. Day-by-day, you're taking the steps to get stronger, more heart healthy, and more flexible. It means day-by-day commitment and consistent work on your part. There may have been times when you've experienced some discomfort. I did, too, when I first stepped out of my comfort zone.

I know it's not easy. I also know that to be truly healthy, you can't focus on exercise alone. You must review your diet and examine what you choose to consume on a regular basis! And I'm not talking about sweet coffee drinks, pizza, and beer—well, not completely.

In part four of *Civility Unleashed*, we looked at what you ingest regularly and how it affects your attitudes and behavior toward others. Remember, the focus on our civil selves is two-fold: how we exercise civility toward others and how we exercise civility toward ourselves. The reason that's critical to your success in the development of your civil self is this: it's next to impossible to consistently treat others with civility if you don't consistently treat yourself with civility.

## READY TO TOSS OUT THE GARBAGE?

It's time to scrutinize what's in your emotional and mental pantry and survey the shelves. If what you're taking in isn't serving you well and making your civil self stronger, toss it. If it's nourishing your civil self, keep it. And if you could use a bit more of a specific attitude or know-how, stock up!

In *Civility Unleashed,* we studied eight nasty qualities and behaviors that were as toxic as any chemically laden processed food. Remember, these are behaviors and attitudes that are roadblocks to achieving your best civil self. In other words, they break down your ability to create **trust**—trust by others in you and trust in yourself to consistently respond with civility.

Here are the original eight "junk" attitudes and behaviors from *Civility Unleashed:*

- ☐ **Excuses.** Reasons we come up with for being uncivil
- ☐ **Entitlement.** Self-absorption and self-importance
- ☐ **Rumination.** Chewing over past mistakes
- ☐ **Authenticity.** That rude behavior is "who" I am
- ☐ **Unhealthy choices.** Too little sleep, too much junk-food, too little exercise
- ☐ **Personal intake of garbage.** What are you filling your head with—think about what you watch, listen to, and who you surround yourself with
- ☐ **No systems in place.** Not paying attention to your manners
- ☐ **Ignorance.** Little understanding of what civility is

Double check that these also aren't on your menu:

- ☐ **Poor attitude.** Negative, not positive
- ☐ **Gossip.** It destroys trust
- ☐ **Victim mindset.** The other person is the villain
- ☐ **Ingratitude.** Not grateful or appreciative
- ☐ **Poor language.** Obscenity-laden conversations
- ☐ **Apathy.** You don't care
- ☐ **Negative energy.** What you put out is not healthy or good
- ☐ **Lack of follow-through.** You don't do what you say you're going to do
- ☐ **Inattentiveness to appearance.** You pay no attention that you communicate through your grooming, clothing, and how you carry yourself
- ☐ **Reacting, not responding.** You don't take a breath and pause first

Please review this list and place a check next to those attitudes and behaviors that are barriers to reaching your goal. (This is the goal you chose when you first walked into the civility gym.) Which ones are not aligned with your core values? Those words represent speed bumps to your ability to demonstrate civility toward others—and yourself.

# C's the Day EXERCISE

Select three of the words you checked to focus on for the next two weeks. You're going to work to get them **out** of your mental pantry.

_____

_____

_____

Write recent specific examples when those attitudes or behaviors became hurdles to your moving forward with civility.

_____

_____

_____

_____

_____

How are those three attitudes or behaviors getting in the way of you achieving your goals? How do they put you into a position that is not aligned with your core values?

_____

_____

_____

_____

**Communicating Character by Exercising Civility**

## HEALTHY CHOICES

The last thing I want to do is leave you craving those old negative attitudes and behaviors! Let's determine what you need to stock up on to replace them.

Again, in *Civility Unleashed,* you and I examined eight healthy choices:

- ☐ **Attention.** To others' wants and needs—not just your own
- ☐ **Boundaries.** Define guidelines for others' behavior toward you
- ☐ **Humor.** Lighten up
- ☐ **Perspective.** Understand where the other person is coming from
- ☐ **Healthy choices.** The choices we make to put ourselves into a healthier position
- ☐ **Consistency.** Behaving with civility regularly
- ☐ **Smile.** Make it a frequent action
- ☐ **The best choice ever.** Don't take offense!

You'll want to add these to your diet, too:

- ☐ **Breathe.** Take a deep breath—regularly—before responding
- ☐ **Say no to gossip.** Don't keep gossip alive
- ☐ **Victor mindset.** Don't hand over your personal control to others
- ☐ **Gratitude.** Appreciate others and what they do
- ☐ **Uplifting and clear language.** Speak to build and clarify
- ☐ **Ownership.** Be accountable and responsible
- ☐ **Positive energy.** You light up the room
- ☐ **Follow-through.** You do what you say you're going to do
- ☐ **Attention to appearance.** You're attentive to how you come across
- ☐ **Respond.** You don't react quickly and thoughtlessly. You respond thoughtfully.

Please review this list of ingredients that you want to add to your diet. These are the attitudes and behaviors that you want to display consistently. Check off those you would like to increasingly add to your civil self diet.

# C's the Day EXERCISE

Review your list and write three behaviors that you will specifically focus on over the next two weeks to nourish your civil self:

_____

_____

_____

_____

_____

Write three specific recent experiences in which you either (1) used these qualities to create a civil experience or (2) you could have used these qualities to improve your experience.

_____

_____

_____

_____

_____

How do these three behaviors and results drive you closer to your goal? Do they align with your core values? How?

_____

_____

_____

_____

_____

**Communicating Character by Exercising Civility**

You've cleaned out and re-stocked your emotional and mental pantry. On the next pages, see how well you stick to your diet.

## ACCOUNTABILITY

*"An optimist is a person who starts a new diet on Thanksgiving Day."*

—Irv Kupcinet

This is your opportunity to hold yourself accountable. Or if you're working with a partner, walk through this chart with that person.

You've identified three attitudes or behaviors that you're going to eliminate in order to create habits that strengthen your civil self. Think of it as monitoring those desserts that really aren't on your diet plan!

You've also pinpointed three attitudes or behaviors that will lead you to strengthen your civil self. It's like eating more veggies and salads!

Fill out this chart for two weeks to monitor how you're doing and to identify where you may need more practice.

| Date | Event | What I did | What I would change | What I would not change |
|------|-------|-----------|---------------------|-------------------------|
|      |       |           |                     |                         |
|      |       |           |                     |                         |
|      |       |           |                     |                         |
|      |       |           |                     |                         |
|      |       |           |                     |                         |
|      |       |           |                     |                         |
|      |       |           |                     |                         |
|      |       |           |                     |                         |
|      |       |           |                     |                         |
|      |       |           |                     |                         |
|      |       |           |                     |                         |
|      |       |           |                     |                         |
|      |       |           |                     |                         |

As your **positive and nourishing** attitudes and behaviors become habit, identify and replace any **negative or undermining** attitudes and behaviors you may have with stronger, more positive ones.

## KEEP GOING!

For two weeks, you've committed to a diet—dumping the junk and consuming what's healthy. Those are terrific first steps. Now the Civil Self Diet becomes **exactly** like every other diet plan—it's up to you to stick with it.

Yes, this is the hard part. The excitement has worn off. You didn't wake up after a couple of days on a diet to be able to fit into a pair of slacks with a much smaller waistband, and you probably won't find that after two weeks you will be able to easily handle all obstacles and demanding people. It takes time and attention.

Just like paying attention to every calorie, you must pay attention to the negative behaviors and attitudes you want to ditch as well as the positive and robust qualities you want to nurture and grow.

How? Instead of monitoring every calorie, you monitor your interactions and reactions—internal and external. Notice that when you smile, you feel different. Notice the reactions of those around you. Pay attention to your feelings when you gossip. Then pay attention to who spreads the gossip and its effect on others. Feel what happens inside you when you confront the challenge of change or stress with humor. Observe how that lighter side of you affects those with whom you work.

Pay attention! The act of paying attention will set you on the path to success!

### Music, Meditation, and the Magic of Moments

When you strive to stay on track, remember to cherish your moments of fun, joy, and success. You're more likely to stick to something you enjoy doing.

One of the best ways to be successful on any kind of diet—including the Civil Self Diet—is to add music to the mix. Whether heading to work, on a break, at lunch, or on the way home, crank up the tunes to help you stay the course. Prayer, meditation, and mindfulness can also serve as aids in your journey to success.

What's important to remember is that like any diet, to lose (or even gain) weight, it takes attention, commitment, and work. You're doing wonderfully—keep going!

## Observations

As you become more aware and mindful of you, your environment, and others, take note of insights, surprises, and results. Please take a moment to write them.

_____

_____

_____

_____

_____

# CONCLUSION: YOUR CIVIL LIFE

Your time in the civility gym isn't over. In fact, it's just begun. In the same way that diet and exercise must become an ingrained habit for you to live a healthy life, exercising and practicing civility must also become a way of life for you.

Becoming stronger, more flexible, more in tune with your heart, and more aware of your nutritional intake takes ongoing practice. I'm thrilled that you joined the civility gym and made the ongoing commitment to grow your civil self.

We need your civil self. Every workplace that you touch with your attention to civility will benefit from your dedication. You'll serve your family and friends every time you flex and stretch your civility muscles.

Don't let your workout stop here. This book is for you to use and re-use. Watch how you grow. Pay attention to your setbacks and learn how to turn them into opportunities. You'll grow stronger, more flexible, and more in tune with your heart day by day. You'll also grow healthier by following the Civil Self Diet.

The power of civility will affect you and your world in exciting and wonderful ways. We're all counting on you to *Unleash Civility*!

# ABOUT THE AUTHOR

Diana Damron is a former television anchor and reporter who uses her well-honed skills of communication to transform businesses, organizations, and individuals. Today Diana is a speaker, trainer, and personal and executive coach. Diana spent years in front of the camera and behind the scenes to interview the famous, the infamous, and those who just have a story to tell. After experiencing both the positive and dark sides of work environments, Diana used her skills to develop **The 3 C's** approach to detect what specifically is holding back a company or an individual from achieving success and personal satisfaction. Diana uses Civility, Communication, and Character **(The 3 C's)** to take organizations and individuals from toxic to trusting. Diana also prepares and coaches individuals—whether executive or at-home-entrepreneur—to speak before audiences whether in the board room or on stage. In person, in front of an audience, and in writing, Diana's work is laced with humor. After all, this is the woman who walked right off the runway and fell into the laps of the stunned crowd at a national modeling competition at the Waldorf Astoria in New York City. You can see Diana's TedxTalk on "The Force of Civility" through her website or through YouTube.com. For information on training, keynotes, fees, and availability, please visit Diana's website at **DianaDamron.com** or email her at **Diana@DianaDamron.com.**

# NOTES

# NOTES

# NOTES

# NOTES

Made in the USA
Middletown, DE
12 April 2022